Tab

Introduction 4

Chapter 1 5

Air fryer Breakfast Recipes 5

    Spinach and Onion Frittata 6

    Egg Filled Eggplants 8

    Air Fryer Egg Burrito 10

    Tropical Mexican Casserole 13

    Stuffed Cheese and Chili Paratha 15

    Traditional Potato Bhaji 17

Chapter 2 19

Air Fryer Recipes for Lunch 19

    Air Fryer Chicken Roast 20

    Minced Chicken Stuffed Spring Rolls 22

    Air Fryer Baked Pizza 24

    Baked Tortilla Wrappers 26

    Air Fried Portable Pita Pizza 28

    Fried Shrimp 30

Chapter 3 32

Air Fryer Recipes for Dinner 32

    Avocado Fries 33

    Spicy Chicken Wings 35

    Fried French Beans and Sweet Potatoes 37

    Ground Beef Stuffed Mushrooms 39

    Ground Chicken Stuffed Bell Peppers 41

Chapter 4 43

Air Fryer Meat Recipes 43
　Air Fryer Meatballs 44
　Marinated Rosemary Zest Turkey Breast 46
　Honey Glazed Pork Ribs 48
　Air Fryer Baked Beef and Potatoes 50
　Spicy Masala Boti 52
　Crispy Pork Roast 54
　Hot Shot Factions 56
　Air Fried Beef Barbecue 58
　Rosemary Beef Steaks 60
　Air Fryer Meatloaf 62
　Meatballs Cooked in Tomato Gravy 64
Chapter 5 66
Air Fryer Fish Recipes 66
　Air Fryer Fish Pockets 67
　Tropical Fish Crust 69
　Air Fryer Honey Glazed Fish 71
　Spicy Fish Fingers 73
　Fish and Potato Patties 75
　Fish Kebab Burger 77
　Air Fried Lemon Fish 79
　Air Fried Baked Salmon 81
　Salmon Tikka Boti 83
　Salmon Seekh Kebabs 85
Chapter 6 87
Air Fryer Vegetable Recipes 87
　Air Fryer Crunchy Kale Chips 88

Spicy Potato Wedges 90

Air Fryer Potato Cutlets 92

Sweet Potato Chips 94

Garlic and Thyme Flavoured Roasted Potatoes 96

Air Fryer Hot and Spicy Eggplant Chips 98

Fried Zucchini Sticks 100

Air Fryer Baked Cauliflower 102

Baked Brussels Sprouts 104

Fried Tomatoes with Basil Pesto 106

Chapter 7 108

Air Fryer Dessert Recipes 108

Air Fryer Zebra Cake 109

Delicious Cumin Cookies 111

Air Fryer Baked Nan Khatai 113

Air Fryer Peanut Cookies 115

Vanilla Crackers with Chocolate Chip 117

Wheat Flour Chocolate Chip Crackers 119

Air Fried Chocolate Filled Puff Rolls 121

Hot Pumpkin Muffins 123

Air Fryer Semolina and Pistachio Bites 125

Blueberry Enchanting Muffins 127

Introduction

The air fryer is a modern apparatus that is multipurpose. It brought the comfort and easiness into the world of cooking. This new technology makes it possible to fry, bake, toast, steam, and grill food in a single pot. The other main advantage of this super innovative machinery is to use a very small amount of cooking oil compared to other existing fryers. In this fryer very hot air is used to cook food in a just few minutes in a healthier way, because it only requires a very small amount of oil even for frying food. Plus a drip tray is inserted into which the fryer basket is fitted in order to cook crunchy and pleasantly golden food.

In the air fryer each and every contemporary and traditional dish can be made very easily, like chicken, fish, beef, vegetables, patties, cakes, pastries, meatballs, kebabs, turkey fajitas, cup-cakes, muffins, chips, quiches, cup-cakes, toasts, burgers, macaroni, curly fries, mousses, puddings, scones, biscuits, and much more in a single pot without any mess and with very little effort.

Now you can make each type of healthy food for your friends and family by using an air fryer that cantinas 80% less cholesterol than any other ordinary fryer. This machinery is highly appropriate for those who want to cook food easily in just few minutes and without so much struggle and mess all over in the kitchen counter. You can make food in air fryer comfortably now that was not imaginable before the introduction of this great and the user friendly technology. Moreover, this equipment is very effective to prevent numerous cardiovascular diseases, due to very less amount of cooking oil usage. So cooking in air fryer is indeed a healthier way for those who love fried and toasted foods but are very conscious about the high intake of oil and fats.

Chapter 1

Air fryer Breakfast Recipes

Spinach and Onion Frittata

Preparation time: 10 minutes
Yield: 4 servings

Ingredients
4 eggs, whisked
1 cup spinach, chopped
1 onion, thinly sliced
¼ teaspoon black pepper
½ teaspoon salt
½ cup cheddar cheese, grated

Directions
1. Preheat air fryer at 360 F.
2. In a bowl, add eggs, spinach, onion, and cheese. Mix well.
3. Season with salt and pepper.

4. Pour mixture into air fryer and set timer for 10 minutes.
5. Serve and enjoy.

Calories	110	Sodium	1,344 mg
Total Fat	5 g	Potassium	0 mg
Saturated	1 g	Total Carbs	8 g
Polyunsaturated	0 g	Dietary Fiber	2 g
Monounsaturated	0 g	Sugars	3 g
Trans	0 g	Protein	8 g
Cholesterol	106 mg		
Vitamin A	47%	Calcium	7%
Vitamin C	18%	Iron	11%

Egg Filled Eggplants

Preparation time: 15 minutes
Yield: 2 servings

Ingredients
1 large eggplant, halved
2 eggs
¼ teaspoon black pepper
¼ teaspoon salt
½ teaspoon dill, chopped
2 tablespoons olive oil

Directions
1. Scoop out the inner portion of eggplant and discard it.
2. Brush eggplants with olive oil.
3. Preheat air fryer at 180c.
4. Place eggplants into air fryer after that crack eggs into eggplants and sprinkle with salt and pepper. Cook again for 5 minutes.
5. Now transfer into serving platter and sprinkle dill on top.

6. Serve and enjoy.

Calories	423	Sodium	1,159 mg
Total Fat	26 g	Potassium	0 mg
Saturated	5 g	Total Carbs	34 g
Polyunsaturated	0 g	Dietary Fiber	10 g
Monounsaturated	0 g	Sugars	10 g
Trans	0 g	Protein	15 g
Cholesterol	260 mg		
Vitamin A	0%	Calcium	0%
Vitamin C	0%	Iron	0%

Air Fryer Egg Burrito

Preparation time: 20 minutes
Yield: 7 servings

Ingredients
1 cup all-purpose flour
¼ cup water
1 teaspoon salt
3 eggs, whisked
2 red bell peppers, sliced
1 onion, thinly sliced
¼ teaspoon black pepper

Directions
1. Season egg with ½ teaspoon salt and some pepper.
2. In air fryer pour eggs mixture and let to cook for 6 minutes on 330 F.
3. Now remove from fryer and transfer to cutting board, let to cool a little and cut with sharp knife. Set aside.

4. Meanwhile, in mixing bowl add flour and salt and knead a soft dough with water.
5. Divide dough into 7-8 equal parts and roll out each part into round circle that can fit into fryer basket.
6. Transfer each circle into fryer and let to cook for 7 minutes on 360 F.
7. Make all circles and place aside.
8. Now transfer onion and bell pepper sliced into fryer basket and bake for 6 minutes on 360 F.
9. Now remove from fryer and place aside.
10. Now fill each cooked circle with fried egg and vegetable mixture, and roll up to make a nice burrito.
11. Serve hot hand enjoy.

Calories	425	Sodium	990 mg
Total Fat	24 g	Potassium	386 mg
Saturated	5 g	Total Carbs	38 g
Polyunsaturated	9 g	Dietary Fiber	2 g
Monounsaturated	0 g	Sugars	3 g
Trans	0 g	Protein	13 g
Cholesterol	271 mg		
Vitamin A	19%	Calcium	13%
Vitamin C	14%	Iron	20%

Tropical Mexican Casserole

Preparation time: 10 minutes
Yield: 4 servings

Ingredients
1 package corn kernels, boiled
4-5 tortillas
2 red bell peppers, chopped
1 cup ground turkey
1 onion, chopped
¼ teaspoon black pepper
¼ teaspoon garlic powder
½ teaspoon salt
2 eggs, whisked

Directions
1. Preheat air fryer at 330 degrees.

2. Place tortillas at the bottom of fryer basket, top with ground turkey, bell peppers, corn kernels and season with salt, garlic powder, and pepper.
3. Leave to cook on 360 F for 9 minutes.
4. Now pour eggs on top and cook again for 7 minutes at 330 F.
5. Serve and enjoy.

Calories	380	Sodium	780 mg
Total Fat	16 g	Potassium	0 mg
Saturated	5 g	Total Carbs	48 g
Polyunsaturated	0 g	Dietary Fiber	8 g
Monounsaturated	0 g	Sugars	4 g
Trans	0 g	Protein	12 g
Cholesterol	20 mg		
Vitamin A	8%	Calcium	25%
Vitamin C	4%	Iron	20%

Stuffed Cheese and Chili Paratha

Preparation time: 15 minutes
Yield: 4 servings

Ingredients
2 cups gram flour
½ cup water
½ teaspoon salt
1 cup mozzarella cheese, grated
2 green chilies, chopped
2 tablespoons green coriander, chopped

Directions
1. In a mixing bowl add flour and salt and knead a soft dough with water.

2. Divide dough into 8-10 equal parts and roll out each part into thin round circle.

3. Now place 1 circle at a clean surface and sprinkle some mozzarella cheese, green coriander, and chilies, top

with another circle and press the edges to seal. Make all parathas the same way.

4. Spray some cooking oil in fryer basket and place 2 parathas at one time.
5. Cook for 7 minutes on 360 F.
6. Serve hot hand enjoy.

Calories	270	Sodium	270 mg
Total Fat	13 g	Potassium	0 mg
Saturated	7 g	Total Carbs	37 g
Polyunsaturated	0 g	Dietary Fiber	4 g
Monounsaturated	0 g	Sugars	4 g
Trans	0 g	Protein	4 g
Cholesterol	0 mg		
Vitamin A	0%	Calcium	5%
Vitamin C	0%	Iron	7%

Traditional Potato Bhaji

Preparation time: 18 minutes
Yield: 3 servings

Ingredients
2 oz. potatoes, cut into small cubes
2 small tomatoes, thinly sliced
1 onion, chopped
¼ teaspoon black pepper
¼ teaspoon chili powder
½ teaspoon salt
½ teaspoon cumin power
¼ teaspoon cinnamon powder

Directions
1. Preheat fryer at 360 F.
2. Transfer potatoes into fryer basket and let to cook for 15 minutes.

3. Now add onion, tomatoes, salt, chili powder, cumin powder, pepper, and cinnamon powder. Toss to combine.
4. Now leave to cook again for 8 minutes on 360 F.
5. Serve and enjoy.

Calories	318	Sodium	960 mg
Total Fat	14 g	Potassium	584 mg
Saturated	4 g	Total Carbs	49 g
Polyunsaturated	1 g	Dietary Fiber	7 g
Monounsaturated	3 g	Sugars	13 g
Trans	0 g	Protein	16 g
Cholesterol	40 mg		
Vitamin A	23%	Calcium	14%
Vitamin C	63%	Iron	16%

Chapter 2

Air Fryer Recipes for Lunch

Air Fryer Chicken Roast

Preparation time: 45 minutes
Yield: 6 servings

Ingredients
1 whole chicken
1 cup yogurt
2 tablespoons lemon juice
1 teaspoon black pepper
1 tablespoons garlic paste
¼ teaspoon ginger powder
1 teaspoon cumin powder
½ teaspoon cinnamon powder
½ teaspoon salt

Directions
1. Make a cut on the chicken with a sharp knife so the marinade can be absorbed well.

2. In a mixing bowl, add yogurt, lemon juice, pepper, cumin powder, cinnamon powder, garlic, ginger powder, and salt. Mix to combine.
3. Drizzle this mixture over chicken and rub all over with clean hands.
4. Place chicken into fridge for 20 minutes.
5. Preheat fryer at 360 F.
6. Place marinated chicken into fryer basket and let to cook for 22 minutes.
7. Now transfer to a serving platter and serve.
8. Enjoy.

Calories	1,470	Sodium	4,400 mg
Total Fat	11 g	Potassium	4,470 mg
Saturated	3 g	Total Carbs	188 g
Polyunsaturated	0 g	Dietary Fiber	51 g
Monounsaturated	0 g	Sugars	19 g
Trans	0 g	Protein	185 g
Cholesterol	275 mg		
Vitamin A	30%	Calcium	42%
Vitamin C	30%	Iron	149%

Minced Chicken Stuffed Spring Rolls

Preparation time: 25 minutes
Yield: 8 servings

Ingredients
8-10 roll sheets
1 cup minced chicken
1 onion, chopped
1 green bell pepper, chopped
½ cup cabbage, chopped
¼ teaspoon black pepper
½ teaspoon salt
2 garlic cloves, minced
1 teaspoon olive oil
1 egg, whisked

Directions
1. Heat oil in pan and fry onion with garlic until transparent.
2. Now add minced chicken and fry until no longer pink.

3. Season with salt and pepper.
4. Add in cabbage and bell pepper. Stir fry for 1-2 minutes.
5. Now place 1 roll sheet on clean surface and place 2-3 tablespoons of minute at one edge of sheet.
6. Brush edges with egg and then roll out over filling.
7. Preheat fryer at 360 F.
8. Place rolls into fryer and let to cook for 10 minutes.
9. Serve and enjoy.

Calories	368	Sodium	828 mg
Total Fat	8 g	Potassium	522 mg
Saturated	1 g	Total Carbs	45 g
Polyunsaturated	3 g	Dietary Fiber	3 g
Monounsaturated	0 g	Sugars	5 g
Trans	0 g	Protein	30 g
Cholesterol	221 mg		
Vitamin A	151%	Calcium	9%
Vitamin C	28%	Iron	24%

Air Fryer Baked Pizza

Preparation time: 25 minutes
Yield: 2 servings

Ingredients
2 pita breads
½ cup dried tomatoes
½ cup tomatoes sauce
¼ cup basil leaves
1 cup mozzarella cheese, grated
½ black pepper
½ teaspoon salt
2 eggs
2 tablespoons olive oil

Directions
1. Spread tomato sauce on each pita bread.
2. Place basil leaves and fried tomatoes, sprinkle salt and pepper.
3. Drizzle some drops of olive oil and sprinkle mozzarella cheese.
4. Preheat air fryer at 180c.

5. Transfer pizzas into air fryer and let to cook for 15 minutes.
6. After that crack egg on each pizza and let to cook again for 10 minutes on 200c.
7. Transfer to serving dish and sprinkle more pepper if you like.
8. Serve hot and enjoy.

Calories	236	Sodium	308 mg
Total Fat	11 g	Potassium	0 mg
Saturated	4 g	Total Carbs	0 g
Polyunsaturated	0 g	Dietary Fiber	2 g
Monounsaturated	0 g	Sugars	0 g
Trans	0 g	Protein	0 g
Cholesterol	136 mg		
Vitamin A	0%	Calcium	0%
Vitamin C	0%	Iron	0%

Baked Tortilla Wrappers

Preparation time: 25 minutes
Yield: 4 servings

Ingredients
4-5 tortilla wrappers
1 chicken breast, cut into small pieces
1 cup black beans, boiled
1 cup corn kernels
1 bunch green coriander, chopped
1 cup yogurt
1 cup cream, whipped
¼ teaspoon black pepper
½ teaspoon salt
2 garlic cloves, minced

Directions
1. Heat oil in saucepan and fry garlic until fragrant.
2. Now add chicken and fry until no longer pink.

3. Season with salt and pepper. Transfer to bowl and place aside.
4. In a blender, add yogurt and green coriander, blend till puree. Place aside.
5. Preheat fryer at 360 F.
6. Place tortillas into fryer basket and leave to prepare for 7 minutes.
7. Now remove from fryer and top each tortilla with black beans, chicken, some green sauce, and whipped cream.
8. Serve and enjoy.

Calories	3,367	Sodium	9,956 mg
Total Fat	144 g	Potassium	2,414 mg
Saturated	74 g	Total Carbs	210 g
Polyunsaturated	8 g	Dietary Fiber	6 g
Monounsaturated	7 g	Sugars	53 g
Trans	0 g	Protein	268 g
Cholesterol	990 mg		
Vitamin A	20%	Calcium	45%
Vitamin C	75%	Iron	91%

Air Fried Portable Pita Pizza

Preparation time: 15 minutes
Yield: 2 servings

Ingredients
2 pita breads
1 cup tomato sauce
1 tablespoon thyme
2 green bell pepper, sliced
1 onion, sliced
¼ teaspoon black pepper
1 cup mozzarella cheese, chopped

Directions
1. Place 1 pita bread and spread 4-5 tablespoons of tomato sauce, top with onion and bell pepper slices as much you like.
2. Now sprinkle cheese, thyme, pepper, and repeat the same steps for the second pizza.
3. Preheat fryer at 330 F.

4. Transfer pizzas into air fryer and leave to prepare for 9 minutes.
5. Serve and enjoy.

Calories	1,039	Sodium	937 mg
Total Fat	52 g	Potassium	1,283 mg
Saturated	15 g	Total Carbs	105 g
Polyunsaturated	5 g	Dietary Fiber	25 g
Monounsaturated	25 g	Sugars	7 g
Trans	0 g	Protein	46 g
Cholesterol	412 mg		
Vitamin A	12%	Calcium	8%
Vitamin C	404%	Iron	28%

Fried Shrimp

Preparation time: 15 minutes
Yield: 4 servings

Ingredients
2 oz. shrimp
1 cup bread crumbs
1 egg, whisked
¼ teaspoon black pepper
½ teaspoon salt
1 teaspoon garlic powder

Directions
1. In a bowl add bread crumbs, salt, and black pepper. Mix well.
2. Dip each shrimp into egg then roll into the bread crumb mixture.
3. Preheat fryer at 360 F.

4. Transfer shrimp into fryer basket and let to cook for 10 minutes.
5. Serve and enjoy.

Calories	760	Sodium	930 mg
Total Fat	37 g	Potassium	0 mg
Saturated	7 g	Total Carbs	86 g
Polyunsaturated	0 g	Dietary Fiber	7 g
Monounsaturated	0 g	Sugars	5 g
Trans	1 g	Protein	19 g
Cholesterol	35 mg		
Vitamin A	2%	Calcium	17%
Vitamin C	15%	Iron	16%

Chapter 3

Air Fryer Recipes for Dinner

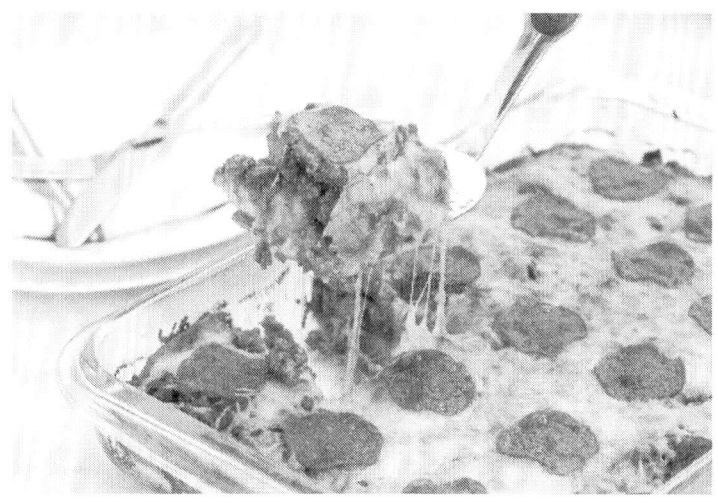

Avocado Fries

Preparation time: 15 minutes
Yield: 4 servings

Ingredients
4 avocados, pitted, 1 inch thick slices
¼ cup all-purpose flour
1 cup bread crumbs
2 eggs, whisked
¼ teaspoon black pepper
1 teaspoon dried thyme
1 teaspoon cinnamon powder
½ teaspoon salt
1 teaspoon garlic powder

Directions
1. Take a bowl and add bread crumbs, cinnamon powder, thyme, salt, and black pepper. Mix well.
2. Dip each avocado slice into egg then roll into flour and then in bread crumbs mixture.

3. Preheat fryer at 360 F.
4. Transfer avocados into fryer basket and let to cook for 15 minutes.
5. Serve and enjoy.

Calories	440	Sodium	294 mg
Total Fat	15 g	Potassium	1,644 mg
Saturated	3 g	Total Carbs	65 g
Polyunsaturated	8 g	Dietary Fiber	7 g
Monounsaturated	3 g	Sugars	4 g
Trans	1 g	Protein	8 g
Cholesterol	5 mg		
Vitamin A	1%	Calcium	5%
Vitamin C	64%	Iron	18%

Spicy Chicken Wings

Preparation time: 15 minutes
Yield: 4 servings

Ingredients
3 oz. chicken wings
½ cup barbecue sauce
½ cup chili garlic sauce
½ teaspoon salt
¼ teaspoon garlic paste
1 teaspoon ginger powder
2 tablespoons lime juice
1 tablespoon olive oil

Directions
1. Take a bowl and add barbecue sauce, chili garlic sauce, garlic paste, ginger powder, salt, lime juice, and oil mix to combine.
1. Transfer chicken wings and mix well until wings are coated with sauce.
2. Preheat air fryer at 360 F.

3. Now place chicken wings into fryer basket as much can fit and let to cook for 22 minutes at 360 F.
4. Serve with desired sauce enjoy.

Calories	210	Sodium	250 mg
Total Fat	7 g	Potassium	125 mg
Saturated	5 g	Total Carbs	24 g
Polyunsaturated	0 g	Dietary Fiber	1 g
Monounsaturated	0 g	Sugars	2 g
Trans	0 g	Protein	18 g
Cholesterol	0 mg		
Vitamin A	20%	Calcium	15%
Vitamin C	20%	Iron	8%

Fried French Beans and Sweet Potatoes

Preparation time: 15 minutes
Yield: 3 servings

Ingredients
2 oz. French beans, trimmed
4-5 sweet potatoes, peeled, thinly sliced
¼ teaspoon black pepper
½ teaspoon salt
¼ teaspoon garlic powder
1 tablespoon olive oil

Directions
1. Transfer French beans and sweet potatoes into fryer basket and drizzle oil, toss to combine.
2. Leave to cook for 9 minutes on 330 F.   170°C
3. Now season with salt, pepper and garlic powder, mix and cook again for 7 minutes on 360 F.   180°C

4. Serve and enjoy.

Calories	2,521	Sodium	9,900 mg
Total Fat	146 g	Potassium	94 mg
Saturated	40 g	Total Carbs	189 g
Polyunsaturated	0 g	Dietary Fiber	2 g
Monounsaturated	1 g	Sugars	122 g
Trans	0 g	Protein	114 g
Cholesterol	480 mg		
Vitamin A	2%	Calcium	37%
Vitamin C	3%	Iron	38%

Ground Beef Stuffed Mushrooms

Preparation time: 35 minutes
Yield: 4 servings

Ingredients
1 cup ground beef
4-5 mushrooms, stems removed
2 tomatoes, chopped
1 onion, chopped
¼ teaspoon black pepper
½ teaspoon salt
2 garlic cloves, minced
2 tablespoons olive oil

Directions
1. Heat oil in saucepan and fry onion until transparent.
2. Now add garlic and beef, fry until no longer pink.
3. Season with salt and pepper.
4. Now add tomatoes and stir fry until tomatoes are softened.
5. Preheat oven at 180c.

6. Fill mushrooms with 2-3 tablespoons of mince mixture and place into air fryer.
7. Leave to prepare for 15 minute.
8. After that cook for 5 minutes on 200c.
9. Serve and enjoy.

Calories	200	Sodium	20 mg
Total Fat	0 g	Potassium	780 mg
Saturated	0 g	Total Carbs	47 g
Polyunsaturated	0 g	Dietary Fiber	0 g
Monounsaturated	0 g	Sugars	42 g
Trans	0 g	Protein	3 g
Cholesterol	0 mg		
Vitamin A	0%	Calcium	0%
Vitamin C	0%	Iron	0%

Ground Chicken Stuffed Bell Peppers

Preparation time: 25 minutes
Yield: 4 servings

Ingredients
2 green bell peppers
2 yellow bell pepper
2 cups ground chicken
1 tomato, chopped
1 onion, chopped
¼ teaspoon black pepper
½ teaspoon salt
2 garlic cloves, minced
½ cup mozzarella cheese, grated
1 tablespoon olive oil

Directions
1. Remove the upper 1 inch slice of bell peppers.
2. Heat oil in saucepan and fry onion until transparent.
3. Now add garlic and chicken, fry till no longer pink.

4. Season with salt and pepper.
5. Now add tomatoes and stir fry till tomatoes are softened.
6. Preheat fryer at 330 F.
7. Fill bell peppers with 3-4 tablespoons of mixture and top with cheese,
8. Transfer into air fryer and leave to prepare for 15 minutes.
9. After that, cook for 5 minutes on 360 F.
10. Serve and enjoy.

Calories	538	Sodium	1,048 mg
Total Fat	3 g	Potassium	1,699 mg
Saturated	0 g	Total Carbs	117 g
Polyunsaturated	1 g	Dietary Fiber	23 g
Monounsaturated	0 g	Sugars	85 g
Trans	0 g	Protein	15 g
Cholesterol	0 mg		
Vitamin A	221%	Calcium	24%
Vitamin C	1,175%	Iron	32%

Chapter 4

Air Fryer Meat Recipes

Air Fryer Meatballs

Preparation time: 10 minutes
Yield: 6 servings

Ingredients
2 cups ground beef
1 bunch coriander leaves, chopped
2 bread slices
1 onion, chopped
¼ teaspoon black pepper
½ teaspoon salt
1 teaspoon garlic pate
1 teaspoon ginger powder
1 teaspoon cumin powder
¼ teaspoon cinnamon powder

Directions
1. In a food processor add beef, bread slices, coriander, salt, pepper, cumin powder, cinnamon powder, and ginger garlic paste. Blend well.

2. Grease your hands with some oil and make small round balls with mixture.
3. Preheat fryer at 360 F.
4. Transfer meatballs into fryer basket and let to cook for 8 minutes on 360 F.
5. After that cook for 5 minutes on 330 F.
6. Serve and enjoy.

Calories	430	Sodium	1,045 mg
Total Fat	14 g	Potassium	35 mg
Saturated	5 g	Total Carbs	17 g
Polyunsaturated	2 g	Dietary Fiber	1 g
Monounsaturated	3 g	Sugars	3 g
Trans	0 g	Protein	31 g
Cholesterol	85 mg		
Vitamin A	6%	Calcium	25%
Vitamin C	6%	Iron	2%

Marinated Rosemary Zest Turkey Breast

Preparation time: 45 minutes
Yield: 4 servings

Ingredients
1 turkey breast
3 tablespoons honey
1 teaspoon garlic powder
¼ teaspoon black pepper
½ teaspoon salt
2 tablespoons rosemary, chopped
2 tablespoons lemon juice
1 teaspoon cinnamon powder

Directions
1. In a medium bowl add, garlic powder, honey, lemon juice, black pepper, cinnamon powder, rosemary, and salt. Mix to combine.

2. Drizzle over turkey breast and toss rub all over gently. Let to marinade for 30 minutes.

3. Preheat air fryer at 360 F.
4. Now place turkey breast into fryer basket as much can fit and let to cook for 22 minutes at 360 F.
5. Transfer to serving platter.
6. Serve and enjoy.

Calories	426	Sodium	219 mg
Total Fat	4 g	Potassium	362 mg
Saturated	1 g	Total Carbs	51 g
Polyunsaturated	1 g	Dietary Fiber	6 g
Monounsaturated	1 g	Sugars	2 g
Trans	0 g	Protein	42 g
Cholesterol	98 mg		
Vitamin A	12%	Calcium	9%
Vitamin C	134%	Iron	14%

Honey Glazed Pork Ribs

Preparation time: 7 minutes
Yield: 6 servings

Ingredients
4 oz. pork ribs
½ cup honey
2 tablespoons soya sauce
1 teaspoon black pepper
½ teaspoon salt
1 teaspoon garlic paste

Directions
1. In a piping bag add honey, soya sauce, black pepper, salt, garlic and pork ribs, shake bag to coat well.
2. Preheat air fryer at 360 F.
3. Transfer pork ribs and leave to cook for 7 minutes.

4. Serve and enjoy.

Calories	295	Sodium	589 mg
Total Fat	23 g	Potassium	6 mg
Saturated	2 g	Total Carbs	8 g
Polyunsaturated	5 g	Dietary Fiber	2 g
Monounsaturated	12 g	Sugars	3 g
Trans	0 g	Protein	14 g
Cholesterol	0 mg		
Vitamin A	60%	Calcium	11%
Vitamin C	6%	Iron	15%

Air Fryer Baked Beef and Potatoes

Preparation time: 15 minutes
Yield: 5 servings

Ingredients
4 oz. beef cut into bite pieces
3 potatoes, peeled, diced
1 onion, sliced
¼ teaspoon chili powder
½ teaspoon salt
2 tablespoons soya sauce
2 garlic cloves, minced
1 tablespoon olive oil
1 tablespoon coriander leaves, chopped

Directions
1. In air fryer add beef, potatoes, garlic, soya sauce, oil, salt and chili powder. Mix to combine.
2. Let to cook for 8 minutes on 360 F.

3. Now add onion and cook again for 8 minutes on 330 F.
4. Transfer to serving dish and sprinkle coriander on top.
5. Serve hot and enjoy.

Calories	227	Sodium	2,376 mg
Total Fat	8 g	Potassium	352 mg
Saturated	2 g	Total Carbs	19 g
Polyunsaturated	2 g	Dietary Fiber	0 g
Monounsaturated	4 g	Sugars	0 g
Trans	0 g	Protein	19 g
Cholesterol	23 mg		
Vitamin A	106%	Calcium	7%
Vitamin C	29%	Iron	22%

Spicy Masala Boti

Preparation time: 35 minutes
Yield: 6 servings

Ingredients

4 oz. beef, boneless, cut into small pieces
1 teaspoon dry coriander powder
1 teaspoon cinnamon powder
1 teaspoon cumin powder
1 teaspoon cayenne pepper
2 tablespoons vinegar
½ teaspoon salt
1 teaspoon garlic powder
1 teaspoon ginger powder
1 teaspoon olive oil

Directions

1. In a bowl add all spices and mix to combine.
2. Transfer beef into fryer and sprinkle all spices, mix well to combine.

3. Now add vinegar and olive oil and toss well.
4. Leave to cook for 15 minutes on 390 F.
5. After that cook for 5 minutes on 360 F.
6. Serve and enjoy.

Calories	568	Sodium	152 mg
Total Fat	42 g	Potassium	760 mg
Saturated	36 g	Total Carbs	96 g
Polyunsaturated	0 g	Dietary Fiber	16 g
Monounsaturated	3 g	Sugars	28 g
Trans	0 g	Protein	8 g
Cholesterol	0 mg		
Vitamin A	1,752%	Calcium	16%
Vitamin C	148%	Iron	16%

Crispy Pork Roast

Preparation time: 10 minutes
Yield: 4 servings

Ingredients
2-3 pork chops
1 tablespoon garlic powder
1 tablespoon ginger powder
1 egg, whisked
1 cup bread crumbs
¼ cup flour
1 teaspoon onion powder
1 teaspoon black pepper
½ teaspoon salt

Directions
1. In a bowl combine flour, breadcrumbs, salt, pepper, ginger powder, garlic powder and onion powder. Mix well.
2. Dip each pork chop into egg then roll out into bread crumbs mixture.

3. Transfer pork into air fryer basket and let to cook for 6 minutes.
4. Flip the sides and now leave to cook for 4 minutes on 150 F.
5. Serve and enjoy.

Calories	158	Sodium	43 mg
Total Fat	14 g	Potassium	247 mg
Saturated	12 g	Total Carbs	10 g
Polyunsaturated	0 g	Dietary Fiber	2 g
Monounsaturated	0 g	Sugars	4 g
Trans	0 g	Protein	1 g
Cholesterol	0 mg		
Vitamin A	5%	Calcium	4%
Vitamin C	11%	Iron	1%

Hot Shot Factions

Preparation time: 22 minutes
Yield: 5 servings

Ingredients
4 oz. beef steaks, cut into 2 inch pieces
½ cup tomato ketchup
2 tablespoons vinegar
2 tablespoons honey
½ teaspoon salt
¼ teaspoon garlic paste
2 tablespoons lime juice

Directions
1. Take a bowl and add, tomato ketchup, honey, garlic paste, salt, and lime juice. Mix to combine.
2. Transfer into air fryer at 360 F for 22 minutes.
3. Serve with desired sauce enjoy.

Calories	158	Sodium	43 mg
Total Fat	14 g	Potassium	247 mg
Saturated	12 g	Total Carbs	10 g
Polyunsaturated	0 g	Dietary Fiber	2 g
Monounsaturated	0 g	Sugars	4 g
Trans	0 g	Protein	1 g
Cholesterol	0 mg		
Vitamin A	5%	Calcium	4%
Vitamin C	11%	Iron	1%

Air Fried Beef Barbecue

Preparation time: 15 minutes

Yield: 4 servings

Ingredients

3 oz. beef cut into 1 inch strips
2 tablespoons soy sauce
1 teaspoon chili flakes
4 tablespoons Worcestershire sauce
¼ teaspoon black pepper
½ teaspoon salt
2 garlic cloves, minced
2 tablespoons olive oil

Directions

1. In a bowl, add soy sauce, chili flakes, Worcestershire sauce, olive oil, black pepper, and salt.
2. Transfer into air fryer for 10 minutes on 360 F.
3. Serve and enjoy.

Calories	833	Sodium	2,529 mg
Total Fat	5 g	Potassium	531 mg
Saturated	1 g	Total Carbs	122 g
Polyunsaturated	1 g	Dietary Fiber	4 g
Monounsaturated	1 g	Sugars	65 g
Trans	0 g	Protein	75 g
Cholesterol	0 mg		
Vitamin A	13%	Calcium	2%
Vitamin C	569%	Iron	19%

Rosemary Beef Steaks

Preparation time: 10 minutes
Yield: 4 servings

Ingredients
2 beef steaks
2 tablespoons soy sauce
2 tablespoons Worcestershire
¼ teaspoon black pepper
½ teaspoon salt
1 tablespoon ginger powder
2 tablespoons dried rosemary

Directions
1. In a bowl add soy sauce, Worcestershire sauce, black pepper, ginger powder, rosemary, olive oil, and salt.
2. Drizzle sauce over steaks and rub all over.
3. Transfer into air fryer for 6 minutes on 360 F.
4. Now cook again for 4 minutes at 150 F.

5. Serve and enjoy.

Calories	18	Sodium	23 mg
Total Fat	1 g	Potassium	4 mg
Saturated	0 g	Total Carbs	2 g
Polyunsaturated	0 g	Dietary Fiber	0 g
Monounsaturated	0 g	Sugars	0 g
Trans	0 g	Protein	2 g
Cholesterol	5 mg		
Vitamin A	1%	Calcium	1%
Vitamin C	0%	Iron	1%

Air Fryer Meatloaf

Preparation time: 15 minutes
Yield: 4 servings

Ingredients
2 cups ground beef
1 cup tomato ketchup
1 teaspoon chili powder
½ teaspoon salt
1 teaspoon garlic paste
½ teaspoon ginger paste

Directions
1. In a food processor add ground beef, 2 bread slices, chili powder, salt, garlic paste, and ginger paste. Blend well.
2. Shape mixture in the form of loaf and transfer on aluminium foil.
3. Pour over tomato ketchups and wrap in foil.
4. Preheat air fryer at 360 F.

5. Transfer load into air fryer and leave to cook for 10 minutes.
6. After that cook for 5 minutes at 330 F.
7. Serve and enjoy.

Calories	46	Sodium	2 mg
Total Fat	0 g	Potassium	170 mg
Saturated	0 g	Total Carbs	11 g
Polyunsaturated	0 g	Dietary Fiber	1 g
Monounsaturated	0 g	Sugars	9 g
Trans	0 g	Protein	1 g
Cholesterol	0 mg		
Vitamin A	17%	Calcium	1%
Vitamin C	21%	Iron	2%

Meatballs Cooked in Tomato Gravy

Preparation time: 15 minutes
Yield: 4 servings

Ingredients
1 cup tomato sauce
2 cups ground beef
2 bread slices
1 onion, chopped
¼ teaspoon black pepper
½ teaspoon salt
2 tablespoons mint leaves, chopped
1 teaspoon garlic pate
1 teaspoon ginger powder
1 teaspoon cumin powder
¼ teaspoon cinnamon powder

Directions
1. In a food processor, add beef, bread slices, mint leaves, salt, pepper, cumin powder, cinnamon powder, and ginger garlic paste. Blend well.

2. Grease your hands with some oil and make small round balls with mixture.
3. Preheat fryer at 360 F.
4. Transfer meatballs into fryer basket and let to cook for 8 minutes on 360 F.
5. Drizzle tomato sauce over meatballs and cook again for 5 minutes on 330 F.
6. Serve and enjoy.

Calories	358	Sodium	1,990 mg
Total Fat	4 g	Potassium	0 mg
Saturated	0 g	Total Carbs	44 g
Polyunsaturated	1 g	Dietary Fiber	7 g
Monounsaturated	0 g	Sugars	9 g
Trans	0 g	Protein	37 g
Cholesterol	70 mg		
Vitamin A	340%	Calcium	8%
Vitamin C	32%	Iron	17%

Chapter 5

Air Fryer Fish Recipes

Air Fryer Fish Pockets

Preparation time: 20 minutes
Yield: 6 servings

Ingredients
1 ½ cup al purpose flour
1 cup ground fish
1 bunch coriander leaves, chopped
1 onion, chopped
¼ teaspoon black pepper
½ teaspoon salt
2 garlic cloves, minced
¼ teaspoon cinnamon powder
¼ cup water
1 tablespoon olive oil

Directions
1. In a mixing bowl add flour and some salt, kneed a soft dough. Place aside for 30 minutes.
2. Heat oil in pan and fry onion with garlic until transparent.
3. Now add in fish and fry for 4-5 minutes.
4. Transfer coriander and toss to combine, place aside.
5. Now divide dough into 6-8 equal parts and roll out each part into ¼ inch thick circle.

6. Brush edges with a little water.
7. Top each circle with 1 tablespoon of mixture and lift one side of circle and flip over the filling to make a pocket.
8. Preheat fryer at 360 F.
9. Now prickle each pocket with folk and transfer into air fryer basket.
10. Let to cook for 8 minutes on 360 F.
11. After that, flip the sides and cook for 5 minutes on 330 F.
12. Serve and enjoy.

Calories	202	Sodium	284 mg
Total Fat	8 g	Potassium	68 mg
Saturated	2 g	Total Carbs	24 g
Polyunsaturated	1 g	Dietary Fiber	5 g
Monounsaturated	3 g	Sugars	3 g
Trans	0 g	Protein	11 g
Cholesterol	210 mg		
Vitamin A	7%	Calcium	7%
Vitamin C	0%	Iron	13%

Tropical Fish Crust

Preparation time: 12 minutes
Yield: 4 servings

Ingredients
2 fish fillets, cut into half pieces
½ cup flour
1 egg, whisked
½ cup bread crumbs
1 teaspoon black pepper
½ teaspoon salt
1 teaspoon garlic powder
1 teaspoon onion powder

Directions
1. In a bowl add flour, salt, pepper, garlic powder, and onion powder, mix well.
2. Dip each fish piece into egg, then roll out into flour and then into bread crumbs.
3. Preheat air fryer at 360 F.
4. Transfer fish pieces and leave to cook for 12 minutes.
5. Serve and enjoy.

Calories	130	Sodium	690 mg
Total Fat	3 g	Potassium	450 mg
Saturated	1 g	Total Carbs	17 g
Polyunsaturated	0 g	Dietary Fiber	2 g
Monounsaturated	0 g	Sugars	4 g
Trans	0 g	Protein	9 g
Cholesterol	15 mg		
Vitamin A	20%	Calcium	2%
Vitamin C	0%	Iron	2%

Air Fryer Honey Glazed Fish

Preparation time: 12 minutes
Yield: 4 servings

Ingredients
3-4 fish fillets
¼ cup honey
1 teaspoon black pepper
½ teaspoon salt
2 tablespoons soya sauce
1 teaspoon garlic powder
1 tablespoon olive oil

Directions
1. In a bowl add honey, soya sauce, salt, pepper, garlic powder, and olive oil, mix well.
2. Dip each fish piece into mixture and then transfer into fryer basket.
3. Let to cook for 10-12 minutes on 360 F.
4. Serve hot and enjoy.

Calories	145	Sodium	15 mg
Total Fat	7 g	Potassium	612 mg
Saturated	1 g	Total Carbs	17 g
Polyunsaturated	1 g	Dietary Fiber	2 g
Monounsaturated	5 g	Sugars	15 g
Trans	0 g	Protein	2 g
Cholesterol	0 mg		
Vitamin A	43%	Calcium	4%
Vitamin C	81%	Iron	7%

Spicy Fish Fingers

Preparation time: 15 minutes
Yield: 6 servings

Ingredients
2-3 fish fillets, cut into 1 inch strips
1 teaspoon cinnamon powder
1 teaspoon cumin powder
1 teaspoon cayenne pepper
½ teaspoon salt
1 teaspoon garlic powder
1 teaspoon mustard powder
1 teaspoon ginger powder
1 cup bread crumbs
2 eggs, whisked

Directions
1. In a bowl add all spices and mix to combine.
2. Dip each fish finger into eggs then roll out into bread crumbs well.
3. Put finger into fryer basket and leave to cook for 15 minutes on 390 F.
4. Serve and enjoy.

Calories	215	Sodium	439 mg
Total Fat	8 g	Potassium	68 mg
Saturated	2 g	Total Carbs	25 g
Polyunsaturated	1 g	Dietary Fiber	5 g
Monounsaturated	3 g	Sugars	4 g
Trans	0 g	Protein	15 g
Cholesterol	215 mg		
Vitamin A	7%	Calcium	7%
Vitamin C	0%	Iron	12%

Fish and Potato Patties

Preparation time: 15 minutes
Yield: 4 servings

Ingredients
1 cup ground fish
3-4 potatoes, boiled, peeled
1 bunch coriander leaves, chopped
5-6 mint leaves, chopped
¼ teaspoon chili powder
½ teaspoon salt
¼ teaspoon cinnamon powder
½ teaspoon cumin powder
1 tablespoon olive oil

Directions
1. In a mixing bowl add potatoes, mint leaves, coriander leaves, fish, chili powder, salt, cumin powder, and cinnamon powder, mash with potato masher.
2. Now take 2-3 tablespoons of mixture into hand and make round patties.
3. Preheat fryer at 360 F and spray with oil.
4. Now place patties into air fryer basket and allow it cook for 10 minutes on 360 F.

5. After that flip the sides and cook for 5 minutes on 330 F.
6. Serve and enjoy.

Calories	242	Sodium	348 mg
Total Fat	15 g	Potassium	179 mg
Saturated	3 g	Total Carbs	18 g
Polyunsaturated	7 g	Dietary Fiber	1 g
Monounsaturated	5 g	Sugars	2 g
Trans	0 g	Protein	9 g
Cholesterol	26 mg		
Vitamin A	1%	Calcium	2%
Vitamin C	0%	Iron	22%

Fish Kebab Burger

Preparation time: 20 minutes
Yield: 5 servings

Ingredients
1 fish fillet, cut into 2 pieces
½ teaspoon salt
1 teaspoon black pepper
1 cup bread crumbs
1 egg, whisked
1 teaspoon garlic powder
2 cheese slices
2 buns, cut from center
1 cup cream, whipped
½ cup pineapple chunks
1 tablespoons lemon juice

Directions
1. In a platter add crumbs, salt, pepper, and garlic powder, mix well.
2. Dip each fish finger into eggs then roll out into bread crumbs.
3. Transfer fish into fryer basket and leave to cook for 15 minutes on 360 F.

4. Meanwhile in a bowl add cream, lemon juice, and pineapple chunks, mix well.
5. Transfer buns into preheated fryer for 2 minutes, place aside.
6. Now place cheese slice then fried kebab on the base of bun and place a puddle of cream mixture.
7. Top with the cover of buns and serve hot.

Calories	525	Sodium	1,185 mg
Total Fat	8 g	Potassium	370 mg
Saturated	2 g	Total Carbs	61 g
Polyunsaturated	1 g	Dietary Fiber	10 g
Monounsaturated	2 g	Sugars	0 g
Trans	0 g	Protein	31 g
Cholesterol	39 mg		
Vitamin A	3%	Calcium	3%
Vitamin C	25%	Iron	19%

Air Fried Lemon Fish

Preparation time: 15 minutes
Yield: 4 servings

Ingredients
2 fish fillets
½ cup flour
1 tablespoon butter
½ cup coconut milk
2 tablespoons lemon juice
¼ teaspoon white pepper
½ teaspoon salt
2 tablespoons parsley, chopped

Directions
1. Sprinkle salt, and pepper on fish and drizzle lemon juice, toss to coat well.
2. Transfer into air fryer for 10 minutes on 360 F.
3. In a saucepan melt butter and add flour, stir continuously for 1-2 minutes on medium flame.
4. Now add milk and stir well until a thick paste is formed.
5. Transfer fish into platter and drizzle sauce over fish.
6. Sprinkle chopped parsley.

Calories	371	Sodium	424 mg
Total Fat	5 g	Potassium	65 mg
Saturated	0 g	Total Carbs	63 g
Polyunsaturated	0 g	Dietary Fiber	2 g
Monounsaturated	0 g	Sugars	49 g
Trans	0 g	Protein	19 g
Cholesterol	10 mg		
Vitamin A	20%	Calcium	78%
Vitamin C	0%	Iron	4%

Air Fried Baked Salmon

Preparation time: 10 minutes
Yield: 2 servings

Ingredients
1 fillet
1 cup flour
1 egg, whisked
½ cup bread crumbs
1 teaspoon black pepper
½ teaspoon salt
1 teaspoon garlic powder
1 teaspoon ginger powder

Directions
1. In a bowl add flour, salt, pepper, bread crumbs, ginger powder and garlic powder, mix well.
2. Dip each fish piece into egg, then roll out into flour mixture.
3. Preheat air fryer at 360 F.
4. Transfer fish pieces and leave to cook for 10 minutes.
5. Serve and enjoy.

Calories	520	Sodium	744 mg
Total Fat	22 g	Potassium	253 mg
Saturated	10 g	Total Carbs	41 g
Polyunsaturated	0 g	Dietary Fiber	7 g
Monounsaturated	0 g	Sugars	15 g
Trans	0 g	Protein	41 g
Cholesterol	55 mg		
Vitamin A	40%	Calcium	6%
Vitamin C	9%	Iron	6%

Salmon Tikka Boti

Preparation time: 15 minutes
Yield: 6 servings

Ingredients
3 salmon fillets, cut into 1 inch pieces
1 cup yogurt
¼ teaspoon salt
¼ teaspoon turmeric powder
½ teaspoon cayenne pepper
½ teaspoon cinnamon powder
¼ teaspoon cumin powder
¼ teaspoon dry coriander powder
1 tablespoon olive oil

Directions
1. In a bowl add yogurt, salt, pepper, cayenne pepper, cumin powder, turmeric powder, dry coriander powder and cinnamon powder, mix well.
2. Transfer fish pieces into mixture and mix to coat well.
3. Transfer fish pieces into fryer basket and leave to cook for 10 minutes on 360 F.
4. Now brush fish with some oil and leave to cook again for 5 minutes on 330 F.

5. Serve with desired sauce and enjoy.

Calories	453	Sodium	537 mg
Total Fat	7 g	Potassium	718 mg
Saturated	0 g	Total Carbs	58 g
Polyunsaturated	0 g	Dietary Fiber	1 g
Monounsaturated	0 g	Sugars	23 g
Trans	0 g	Protein	22 g
Cholesterol	19 mg		
Vitamin A	121%	Calcium	3%
Vitamin C	30%	Iron	3%

Salmon Seekh Kebabs

Preparation time: 20 minutes
Yield: 4 servings

Ingredients
2 cups salmon, pieces
1 bread slice
3 tablespoons gram flour
¼ teaspoon chili powder
½ teaspoon salt
2 tablespoons coriander leaves, chopped
½ teaspoon garlic paste
2 tablespoons lemon juice

Directions
1. In a food processor add fish, coriander leaves, salt, chili powder, lemon juice, bread slice and gram flour, pulse for 3-4 times till everything is mashed.
2. Now transfer mixture into bowl and take 3-4 tablespoons of mixture into hand and wrap it around the skewer and give it a cylindrical shape by pressing it gently around skewer.
3. Remove carefully from skewer and place into fryer basket.

4. Do same proses for all kebabs on skewers.
5. Put into fryer basket and leave to cook for 10 minutes on 360 F, after that flip the sides and cook for 5 minutes on 390 F.
6. Serve hot with desired sauce.

Calories	525	Sodium	1,185 mg
Total Fat	8 g	Potassium	370 mg
Saturated	2 g	Total Carbs	61 g
Polyunsaturated	1 g	Dietary Fiber	10 g
Monounsaturated	2 g	Sugars	0 g
Trans	0 g	Protein	31 g
Cholesterol	39 mg		
Vitamin A	3%	Calcium	3%
Vitamin C	25%	Iron	19%

Chapter 6

Air Fryer Vegetable Recipes

Air Fryer Crunchy Kale Chips

Preparation time: 10 minutes
Yield: 4 servings

Ingredients

2 bunch kale leaves
1 pinch salt
3-4 tablespoons honey
1 tablespoons olive oil

Directions

1. Preheat fryer at 360 F.
2. Transfer kale leave into fryer basket and let to cook for 10 minutes on 360 F.
3. Now place it in a serving dish and sprinkle some salt on it.
4. Drizzle honey while serving.
5. Serve and enjoy.

Calories	349	Sodium	360 mg
Total Fat	14 g	Potassium	0 mg
Saturated	2 g	Total Carbs	42 g
Polyunsaturated	2 g	Dietary Fiber	8 g
Monounsaturated	0 g	Sugars	14 g
Trans	0 g	Protein	18 g
Cholesterol	0 mg		
Vitamin A	4%	Calcium	0%
Vitamin C	0%	Iron	12%

Spicy Potato Wedges

Preparation time: 10 minutes
Yield: 3 servings

Ingredients
4-5 potato, cut into wedges
3 tablespoons corn flour
½ teaspoon chili powder
1 teaspoon cinnamon powder
½ teaspoon cumin powder
¼ teaspoon black pepper
½ teaspoon salt
1 tablespoon lemon juice
1 teaspoon olive oil

Directions
1. Sprinkle flour on potato wedges and toss to combine.
2. Preheat air fryer at 360 F.
3. Transfer potatoes into fryer basket and drizzle oil, leave to cook for 8 minutes on 360 F.
4. In a bowl add salt, chili powder, cinnamon powder, cumin powder, and black pepper, mix and sprinkle on potatoes, cook again for 2 minutes.
5. Now transfer to serving dish and drizzle lemon juice.

6. Serve and enjoy.

Calories	344	Sodium	578 mg
Total Fat	5 g	Potassium	451 mg
Saturated	2 g	Total Carbs	47 g
Polyunsaturated	2 g	Dietary Fiber	5 g
Monounsaturated	3 g	Sugars	3 g
Trans	0 g	Protein	33 g
Cholesterol	50 mg		
Vitamin A	44%	Calcium	10%
Vitamin C	27%	Iron	21%

Air Fryer Potato Cutlets

Preparation time: 15 minutes
Yield: 5 servings

Ingredients
5-6 large potatoes, boiled, peeled
1 onion, chopped
3 tablespoons green coriander, chopped
1 teaspoon chili powder
½ teaspoon cinnamon powder
½ teaspoon cumin powder
½ teaspoon salt

Directions
1. In a bowl add potatoes, onion, coriander, chili powder, cinnamon powder, cinnamon powder, cumin powder and salt, mash with a potatoes masher.
2. Now make round patties with mixture and place into fryer basket.
3. Let to cook for 10 minutes on 360 F.
4. Transfer to serving dish and sprinkle some coriander on top.
5. Serve hot and enjoy.

Calories	120	Sodium	1,380 mg
Total Fat	5 g	Potassium	0 mg
Saturated	2 g	Total Carbs	7 g
Polyunsaturated	0 g	Dietary Fiber	3 g
Monounsaturated	0 g	Sugars	2 g
Trans	0 g	Protein	9 g
Cholesterol	30 mg		
Vitamin A	0%	Calcium	4%
Vitamin C	110%	Iron	4%

Sweet Potato Chips

Preparation time: 15 minutes
Yield: 6 servings

Ingredients
4-5 sweet potatoes, peeled, cut into 1 inch slices
1 teaspoon cumin seeds, crushed
¼ teaspoon black pepper
½ teaspoon salt

Directions
1. In a bowl potatoes, cumin seeds, salt and pepper, toss to combine.
2. Transfer into fryer and leave to cook for 15 minutes on 390 F.
3. Serve and enjoy.

Calories	1,208	Sodium	479 mg
Total Fat	56 g	**Potassium**	611 mg
Saturated	19 g	**Total Carbs**	131 g
Polyunsaturated	2 g	**Dietary Fiber**	20 g
Monounsaturated	17 g	**Sugars**	13 g
Trans	0 g	**Protein**	60 g
Cholesterol	0 mg		
Vitamin A	43%	Calcium	0%
Vitamin C	159%	Iron	0%

Garlic and Thyme Flavoured Roasted Potatoes

Preparation time: 15 minutes
Yield: 6 servings

Ingredients
2 oz. baby potatoes, halved
2 tablespoons thyme, chopped
2 tablespoons garlic powder
1 teaspoon black pepper
½ teaspoon salt
1 tablespoon olive oil
1 tablespoon lime juice

Directions
1. In a large bowl combine potatoes, olive oil, thyme, salt, pepper, and garlic powder, mix well.
2. Transfer potatoes into air fryer basket and allow it cook for 15 minutes.
3. Serve and enjoy.

Calories	672	Sodium	699 mg
Total Fat	9 g	Potassium	685 mg
Saturated	2 g	Total Carbs	36 g
Polyunsaturated	3 g	Dietary Fiber	3 g
Monounsaturated	4 g	Sugars	3 g
Trans	0 g	Protein	4 g
Cholesterol	2 mg		
Vitamin A	8%	Calcium	4%
Vitamin C	37%	Iron	3%

Air Fryer Hot and Spicy Eggplant Chips

Preparation time: 12 minutes
Yield: 5 servings

Ingredients

2-3 medium eggplants, thinly sliced
2 tablespoons gram flour
¼ teaspoon turmeric powder
½ teaspoon cayenne pepper
1 teaspoon cinnamon powder
½ teaspoon cumin powder
½ teaspoon salt

Directions

1. In a bowl, add salt, flour, cayenne pepper, cinnamon powder and cumin powder, mix and sprinkle on eggplant slices and toss to combine.
2. Preheat air fryer at 360 F.
3. Transfer eggplant slices into fryer basket and leave to cook for 8 minutes on 360 F.
4. After that cook for 4 minutes on 330 F.
5. Serve and enjoy.

Calories	536	Sodium	1,223 mg
Total Fat	11 g	Potassium	631 mg
Saturated	5 g	Total Carbs	80 g
Polyunsaturated	2 g	Dietary Fiber	27 g
Monounsaturated	1 g	Sugars	16 g
Trans	1 g	Protein	33 g
Cholesterol	1 mg		
Vitamin A	30%	Calcium	40%
Vitamin C	40%	Iron	9%

Fried Zucchini Sticks

Preparation time: 15 minutes
Yield: 4 servings

Ingredients
3 large zucchinis, cut into 1 inch slices
1 cup bread crumbs
1 teaspoon chili flakes
¼ teaspoon black pepper
½ teaspoon salt
1 teaspoon garlic powder
½ teaspoon parsley, chopped
1 egg, whisked

Directions
1. In a bowl add bread crumbs, chili powder, garlic powder, salt, parsley and black pepper, mix well.
2. Now dip each zucchini slice into egg then roll into bread crumbs.
3. Transfer into air fryer and cook for 10 minutes on 360 F.
4. After that, cook for 5 minutes on 330 F.
5. Serve and enjoy.

Calories	499	Sodium	975 mg
Total Fat	13 g	Potassium	8 mg
Saturated	1 g	Total Carbs	66 g
Polyunsaturated	0 g	Dietary Fiber	10 g
Monounsaturated	0 g	Sugars	12 g
Trans	0 g	Protein	61 g
Cholesterol	90 mg		
Vitamin A	8%	Calcium	14%
Vitamin C	17%	Iron	22%

Air Fryer Baked Cauliflower

Preparation time: 10 minutes
Yield: 4 servings

Ingredients
2 cups cauliflower florets
½ teaspoon cayenne pepper
¼ teaspoon turmeric powder
½ teaspoon salt
¼ teaspoon cinnamon powder
1 tablespoon olive oil

Directions
1. Preheat fryer at 360 F.
2. In a bowl add olive oil, cayenne pepper, cinnamon powder, turmeric powder and salt, mix to combine.
3. Transfer cauliflower into fryer and leave to cook for 10 minutes on 3360 F.
4. Serve with desired sauce.

Calories	744	Sodium	935 mg
Total Fat	20 g	Potassium	40 mg
Saturated	3 g	Total Carbs	70 g
Polyunsaturated	2 g	Dietary Fiber	3 g
Monounsaturated	1 g	Sugars	51 g
Trans	0 g	Protein	71 g
Cholesterol	224 mg		
Vitamin A	13%	Calcium	12%
Vitamin C	108%	Iron	19%

Baked Brussels Sprouts

Preparation time: 15 minutes
Yield: 4 servings

Ingredients
3 oz. Brussels sprouts
¼ teaspoon black pepper
3 tablespoons soya sauce
½ teaspoon black pepper
¼ teaspoon salt
1 tablespoon olive oil

Directions
1. Preheat fryer at 330 F.
2. Remove the stems and yellow leaves of Brussels sprouts and cut from centre.
3. In a bowl add Brussels sprouts, olive oil, soya sauce, pepper, and salt, toss to coat well.
4. Transfer Brussels into fryer basket and allow it cook for 15 minutes.
5. Serve and enjoy.

Calories	831	Sodium	2,978 mg
Total Fat	51 g	**Potassium**	110 mg
Saturated	13 g	Total Carbs	23 g
Polyunsaturated	17 g	Dietary Fiber	3 g
Monounsaturated	11 g	**Sugars**	7 g
Trans	0 g	**Protein**	79 g
Cholesterol	244 mg		
Vitamin A	8%	Calcium	31%
Vitamin C	8%	Iron	5%

Fried Tomatoes with Basil Pesto

Preparation time: 10 minutes
Yield: 4 servings

Ingredients
2 cups tomatoes, slices
1 cup basil leaves
1 green chili
2 tablespoons honey
½ teaspoon salt
1 teaspoon garlic pate
1 teaspoon olive oil
2 tablespoons lemon juice

Directions
1. In a blender add basil leaves, honey, lemon juice, oil, green chili, salt and garlic paste, and blend well.
2. Transfer to bowl and combine with tomatoes, toss well.
3. Preheat fryer at 360 F.
4. Transfer tomatoes into fryer basket and allow it cook for 10 minutes on 360 F.
5. Serve and enjoy.

Calories	395	Sodium	250 mg
Total Fat	9 g	Potassium	620 mg
Saturated	0 g	Total Carbs	75 g
Polyunsaturated	0 g	Dietary Fiber	4 g
Monounsaturated	0 g	Sugars	71 g
Trans	0 g	Protein	3 g
Cholesterol	0 mg		
Vitamin A	97%	Calcium	0%
Vitamin C	36%	Iron	12%

Chapter 7

Air Fryer Dessert Recipes

Air Fryer Zebra Cake

Preparation time: 20 minutes
Yield: 6 servings

Ingredients
2 cups all-purpose flour
¼ cup butter
½ cup caster sugar
½ teaspoon vanilla essence
1 pinch salt
1 teaspoon baking powder
¼ teaspoon baking soda
2 tablespoons yogurt
2 cups milk
½ cup cocoa powder
4 eggs

Directions
1. Take a mixing bowl and beat eggs until fluffy.
2. Now add butter and beat for 3-4 minutes.
3. Now add in sugar and beat again for 2-3 minutes.
4. Now add flour, salt, baking powder, baking soda, yogurt and vanilla, mix well.
5. Now add milk and beat mixture for 3-4 minutes.

6. Now divide mixture into tow bowls and add cocoa powder in one part, mix well.
7. Preheat fryer at 360 F.
8. Place butter paper into baking mould.
9. Transfer plane mixture into cake dish and then cocoa powder mixture, mix a little with folk and place into air fryer.
10. Allow it cook for 15 minutes on 360 F.
11. After that, cook for 5 minutes on 330 F.
12. Serve and enjoy.

Calories	1,976	Sodium	2,348 mg
Total Fat	64 g	Potassium	343 mg
Saturated	18 g	Total Carbs	260 g
Polyunsaturated	0 g	Dietary Fiber	12 g
Monounsaturated	1 g	Sugars	19 g
Trans	0 g	Protein	65 g
Cholesterol	184 mg		
Vitamin A	14%	Calcium	15%
Vitamin C	0%	Iron	63%

Delicious Cumin Cookies

Preparation time: 12 minutes
Yield: 6 servings

Ingredients
1 ½ cups all-purpose flour
2 tablespoons cumin seeds, crushed
4 tablespoons butter
½ cup caster sugar
½ teaspoon vanilla essence
1 teaspoon baking powder
1 cup coconut milk
2 eggs

Directions
1. Take a mixing bowl and add flour, milk, cumin seeds, caster sugar, baking powder, butter, vanilla essence and eggs, mix well and knead a hard dough.

2. Roll out dough into 1 inch thick sheet and cut with cookie cutter.
3. Preheat fryer at 360 F.

4. Transfer cookies into air fryer and allow it cook for 12 minutes on 360 F.
5. Serve and enjoy.

Calories	380	Sodium	368 mg
Total Fat	6 g	Potassium	650 mg
Saturated	1 g	Total Carbs	65 g
Polyunsaturated	0 g	Dietary Fiber	6 g
Monounsaturated	0 g	Sugars	43 g
Trans	0 g	Protein	21 g
Cholesterol	5 mg		
Vitamin A	20%	Calcium	55%
Vitamin C	52%	Iron	25%

Air Fryer Baked Nan Khatai

Preparation time: 15 minutes
Yield: 7 servings

Ingredients
1 cup semolina
¼ cup all-purpose flour
1 green cardamom, seeds
¼ cup oil
¼ cup caster sugar
¼ teaspoon salt
¼ cup water
1 egg, whisked
Few almonds

Directions
1. In a mixing bowl add semolina, flour, cardamom seeds, oil, sugar and salt, mix well and kneed a hard dough with water.
2. Now take 3-4 tablespoons of mixture into hand and make round cookie by pressing it.
3. Transfer cookies into air fryer, place almond on each cookie by pressing it a little, and brush with egg.
4. Allow it cook for 15 minutes on 360 F.
5. Serve hot and enjoy.

Calories	798	Sodium	229 mg
Total Fat	12 g	Potassium	281 mg
Saturated	3 g	Total Carbs	138 g
Polyunsaturated	4 g	Dietary Fiber	5 g
Monounsaturated	4 g	Sugars	26 g
Trans	0 g	Protein	34 g
Cholesterol	210 mg		
Vitamin A	17%	Calcium	15%
Vitamin C	0%	Iron	37%

Air Fryer Peanut Cookies

Preparation time: 15 minutes
Yield: 6 servings

Ingredients
2 cups all-purpose flour
½ cup peanuts
2 tablespoons semolina
¼ cup brown sugar
1 tablespoon vanilla essence
4 teaspoons olive oil
¼ cup milk

Directions
1. In a bowl, add flour, semolina, sugar, vanilla essence, milk and oil, toss to combine.
2. Now make round cookies with mixture and place a peanut on each cookie.
3. Put cookies into fryer and leave to cook for 15 minutes on 360 F.
4. Serve and enjoy.

Calories	315	Sodium	493 mg
Total Fat	6 g	Potassium	0 mg
Saturated	2 g	Total Carbs	22 g
Polyunsaturated	1 g	Dietary Fiber	4 g
Monounsaturated	1 g	Sugars	22 g
Trans	1 g	Protein	24 g
Cholesterol	0 mg		
Vitamin A	202%	Calcium	4%
Vitamin C	305%	Iron	6%

Vanilla Crackers with Chocolate Chip

Preparation time: 10 minutes
Yield: 6 servings

Ingredients
2 cups all-purpose flour
½ cup chocolate chips
4 tablespoons butter
½ cup caster sugar
1 teaspoon vanilla essence
1 teaspoon baking powder
1 cup coconut milk
2 tablespoons coconut powder
2 eggs

Directions
1. Take a mixing bowl and add flour, milk, coconut powder, caster sugar, baking powder, butter, vanilla essence and eggs, mix well and knead a hard dough.
2. Now add in chocolate chips and mix well.
3. Roll out dough into 1 inch thick sheet and cut with cookie cutter.
4. Preheat fryer at 360 F.

5. Transfer cookies into air fryer and allow it cook for 10 minutes on 360 F.
6. Serve and enjoy.

Calories	1,399	Sodium	1,317 mg
Total Fat	34 g	Potassium	488 mg
Saturated	6 g	Total Carbs	20 g
Polyunsaturated	0 g	Dietary Fiber	0 g
Monounsaturated	0 g	Sugars	12 g
Trans	0 g	Protein	240 g
Cholesterol	905 mg		
Vitamin A	32%	Calcium	15%
Vitamin C	93%	Iron	89%

Wheat Flour Chocolate Chip Crackers

Preparation time: 12 minutes
Yield: 5 servings

Ingredients
2 cups wheat flour
½ cup chocolate chips
¼ cup butter
¼ cup brown sugar
1 teaspoon baking powder
¼ cup almond milk
½ cup chocolate chips
2 eggs

Directions
1. Take a mixing bowl and add flour, milk, sugar, baking powder, chocolate chips, butter and eggs, mix well and knead a hard dough.
2. Preheat fryer at 360 F.
3. Now make round cookies and transfer into air fryer.
4. Allow it cook for 12 minutes on 360 F.
5. Serve and enjoy.

Calories	823	Sodium	156 mg
Total Fat	21 g	**Potassium**	1,958 mg
Saturated	13 g	Total Carbs	63 g
Polyunsaturated	1 g	Dietary Fiber	6 g
Monounsaturated	9 g	Sugars	5 g
Trans	0 g	Protein	29 g
Cholesterol	74 mg		
Vitamin A	8%	**Calcium**	5%
Vitamin C	63%	**Iron**	20%

Air Fried Chocolate Filled Puff Rolls

Preparation time: 15 minutes
Yield: 4 servings

Ingredients
2 puff pastry sheets, cut into 6 equal squares
1 cup chocolate, melted
2 tablespoons butter, melted
2 cups strawberries, chopped
¼ cup coconut powder

Directions
1. Preheat air fryer at 330 F.
2. Combine chocolate and butter.
3. Spread puff pastry pieces on a clean surface and top with 2-3 tablespoons of chocolate then some cowberry chunks.
4. Roll out each sheet and place into a fryer basket.
5. Allow it cook for 10 minutes.
6. After that, change the sides and cook for 5 minutes on 360 F.
7. Serve and enjoy.

Calories	110	Sodium	40 mg
Total Fat	2 g	Potassium	0 mg
Saturated	0 g	Total Carbs	22 g
Polyunsaturated	1 g	Dietary Fiber	3 g
Monounsaturated	1 g	Sugars	6 g
Trans	0 g	Protein	2 g
Cholesterol	0 mg		
Vitamin A	0%	Calcium	0%
Vitamin C	90%	Iron	2%

Hot Pumpkin Muffins

Preparation time: 20 minutes
Yield: 4 servings

Ingredients
2 cups all-purpose flour
1 cup pumpkin puree
¼ cup butter
½ cup caster sugar
½ teaspoon vanilla essence
1 pinch salt
1 teaspoon baking powder
¼ teaspoon baking soda
1 cup milk
2 tablespoons cocoa powder
3 eggs

Directions
1. Crack eggs into bowl and beat till it foams.
2. Now add butter and sugar, beat for 3-4 minutes.
3. Add in flour, pumpkin puree, salt, baking powder, cocoa powder, baking soda and vanilla, mix well.
4. Add milk and beat mixture for 3-4 minutes.
5. Preheat fryer at 360 F.

6. Transfer batter into muffin cases and place into air fryer.
7. Allow it cook for 15 minutes on 360 F.
8. After that cook for 5 minutes on 330 F.
9. Serve and enjoy.

Calories	420	Sodium	1,380 mg
Total Fat	35 g	Potassium	74 mg
Saturated	15 g	Total Carbs	4 g
Polyunsaturated	0 g	Dietary Fiber	0 g
Monounsaturated	0 g	Sugars	4 g
Trans	1 g	Protein	27 g
Cholesterol	110 mg		
Vitamin A	12%	Calcium	34%
Vitamin C	6%	Iron	10%

Air Fryer Semolina and Pistachio Bites

Preparation time: 15 minutes
Yield: 4 servings

Ingredients
2 cups semolina
½ cup all-purpose flour
Few pistachios
¼ cup butter, melted
¼ cup caster sugar
¼ cup warm water

Directions
1. In a mixing bowl add semolina, flour, butter, and sugar, mix well and kneed a hard dough with milk.
2. Now take 3-4 tablespoons of mixture into hand and make round cookies by pressing it.
3. Transfer cookies into air fryer, place pistachio on each cookie by pressing it a little.
4. Allow it cook for 15 minutes on 360 F.
5. Serve hot and enjoy.

Calories	1,527	Sodium	2,199 mg
Total Fat	33 g	Potassium	210 mg
Saturated	12 g	Total Carbs	233 g
Polyunsaturated	0 g	Dietary Fiber	7 g
Monounsaturated	0 g	Sugars	98 g
Trans	0 g	Protein	68 g
Cholesterol	555 mg		
Vitamin A	18%	Calcium	6%
Vitamin C	0%	Iron	12%

Blueberry Enchanting Muffins

Preparation time: 15 minutes
Yield: 6 servings

Ingredients
2 cups all-purpose flour
½ teaspoon baking powder
1 pinch salt
3 tablespoons oil
½ cup milk
1 cup blueberries
½ cup caster sugar

Directions
1. In a bowl add flour, salt, oil, milk, baking powder, sugar and mix well.
2. Fold in blueberries.
3. Pour this batter into greased muffin cases.
4. Place into fryer for 15 minutes at 360 F.
5. Serve and enjoy.

Calories	730	Sodium	875 mg
Total Fat	50 g	Potassium	170 mg
Saturated	9 g	Total Carbs	34 g
Polyunsaturated	1 g	Dietary Fiber	32 g
Monounsaturated	4 g	Sugars	0 g
Trans	0 g	Protein	50 g
Cholesterol	44 mg		
Vitamin A	4%	Calcium	63%
Vitamin C	0%	Iron	19%

Thank you

for buying our book!

I hope Air Fryer Cookbook is helpful for you!
I am constantly looking for way to improve my content to give readers the best value so If you didn't like the book I would like to also hear from you! Please feel free to give your honest opinions as this could help me make improvements.

Finally, if you enjoyed this book, would you be kind enough to leave a review for this book on Amazon?

Thank you and good luck!

Copyright: Published in the United States by Daniel Norton.

All rights Reserved. No part of this publication or the information in it may be quoted from or reproduced in any form by means such as printing, scanning, photocopying or otherwise without prior written permission of the copyright holder.

Disclaimer and Terms of Use: Effort has been made to ensure that the information in this book is accurate and complete, however, the author and the publisher do not warrant the accuracy of the information, text and graphics contained within the book due to the rapidly changing nature of science, research, known and unknown facts and internet. The Author and the publisher do not hold any responsibility for errors, omissions or contrary interpretation of the subject matter herein. This book is presented solely for motivational and informational purposes only

Printed in Great Britain
by Amazon